EASY AND FUN
HIRAGANA

First Steps to Basic Japanese Writing

Author : Kiyomi Ogawa
English Editor : Orrin Cummins

IBC Publishing

Preface

This book is written for people who wish to have fun while learning how to read and write hiragana characters. It has many illustrations, but don't think that it is just for children—I have included many phrases that are widely used in everyday adult life so that the reader can learn not only hiragana but also some useful things to use in conversational Japanese as well.

The Japanese language consists of three different writing systems: hiragana, katakana, and kanji. Hiragana is learned first in school, followed by katakana and then kanji. Difficult kanji characters often have their pronunciations written directly above them to assist readers, a technique known as furigana. This book will show you how to read the furigana that appears in manga, newspapers, and other text.

If writing hiragana is not a priority for you, try the reading exercises. Being able to read literature or manga on your own is a great motivator for advancing your Japanese study. So whatever your immediate goals may be, let's enjoy learning some hiragana!

Kiyomi Ogawa

カバーデザイン：岩目地英樹（コムデザイン）

まえがき

　本書は、ひらがなの読み書きを楽しく勉強したいという方のために書きました。沢山のイラストがあり、一見、子供用の教科書のようですが、大人が日常でよく使う表現の例文をたくさん載せましたので、ひらがなの習得だけではなく日常会話の例文も一緒に学ぶことができるでしょう。

　日本語には3つの文字（ひらがな、カタカナ、漢字）があり、学校ではひらがなを最初に勉強します。次にカタカナ、漢字と学んでいくわけですが、難しい漢字などにはひらがなをふって読みます（振り仮名）。本書では、その振り仮名を使った文章や漫画の読み方も学べるようになっています。

　書くのが苦手な人は読む練習だけでもいいかもしれません。文章や漫画を自分で読めた時の感動は大きいと思います。ぜひ本書で、ひらがなを楽しみながら勉強してくださいね。

小川清美

How to Use This Book

For chapters 2 and 3, practice writing the characters using the correct stroke order.

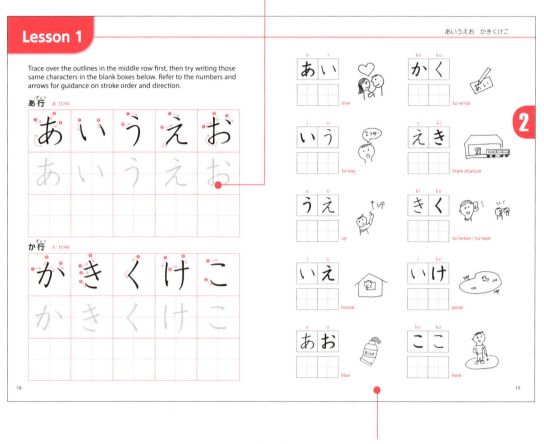

Read and write these words that contain the new characters you just learned.

Learn how to use specific hiragana terms in a sentence in chapter 4.

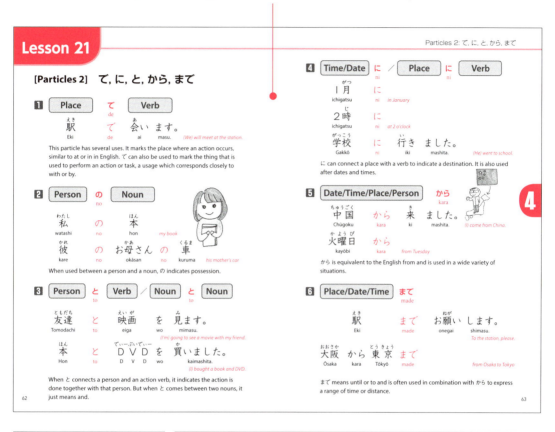

Then in chapter 5, try reading some real-world examples of hiragana.

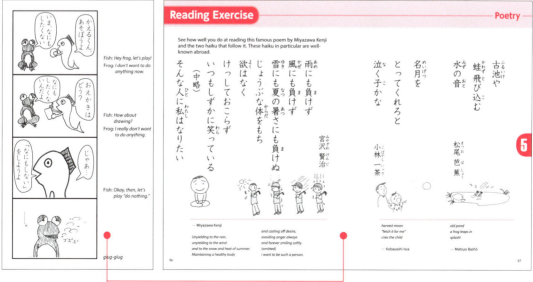

Contents

Preface 2
How to Use This Book 4

Chapter 1 History and Usage ❾
第 1 章　ひらがなの歴史と使われ方

How to Use Hiragana　ひらがなの使われ方 10
The History of Hiragana　ひらがなの歴史 12
Japanese Writing and Pronunciation 14

Chapter 2 Examples and Practice ⓱
Single Characters
第 2 章　ひらがなの書き方

Lesson 1　あいうえお　かきくけこ 18
Lesson 2　さしすせそ　たちつてと 20
Lesson 3　なにぬねの　はひふへほ 22
Lesson 4　まみむめも　やゆよ 24
Lesson 5　らりるれろ　わをん 26
Lesson 6　がぎぐげご　ざじずぜぞ 28
Lesson 7　だぢづでど　ばびぶべぼ 30
Lesson 8　ぱぴぷぺぽ 32
Tricky Characters 34

Chapter 3 Examples and Practice ㊲
Combinations and Symbols
第 3 章　組み合わせた文字・記号

Lesson 9　Small つ 38
Lesson 10　きゃきゅきょ　ぎゃぎゅぎょ 40

Lesson 11	しゃしゅしょ　じゃじゅじょ	42
Lesson 12	ちゃちゅちょ　にゃにゅにょ	44
Lesson 13	ひゃひゅひょ　びゃびゅびょ	46
Lesson 14	ぴゃぴゅぴょ　みゃみゅみょ	48
Lesson 15	りゃりゅりょ　やゆよ＋つ	50
Lesson 16	Extended Vowels	52
Lesson 17	Punctuation 「　」　—　〜	54
Lesson 18	Punctuation 、。	56

Chapter 4 Main Types of Hiragana Words 57
第4章　主にひらがなが使われる言葉

Lesson 19	Greetings and Set Phrases	58
Lesson 20	Particles 1: は, が, を, へ	60
Lesson 21	Particles 2: で, に, と, から, まで	62
Lesson 22	Question Words	64
Lesson 23	Connecting Words	66
Lesson 24	Adverbs	68
Lesson 25	Ideophones	70

Chapter 5 Reading Exercise and the Vertical Style 73
第5章　読む練習・縦書きの練習

Reading Exercise: Adding Kanji	74
Reading Exercise: Adding Kanji	76
Reading Exercise: Adding Katakana	78
Reading Exercise: Longer Passages	80
Reading Exercise: Vertical Writing Style	82
Reading Exercise: Stories and Correspondence	84
Reading Exercise: Poetry	86
Reading Exercise: Manga	88

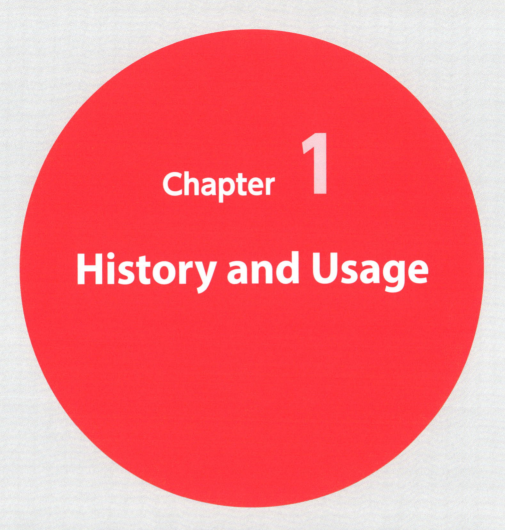

Chapter 1
History and Usage

第 1 章　ひらがなの歴史と使われ方

How to Use Hiragana

The Japanese language consists of three types of characters: hiragana, katakana, and kanji.

Katakana is primarily used for words borrowed from other languages, while kanji is used to write names and parts of verbs and adjectives. Hiragana is used for particles and some parts of verbs and adjectives; it also often appears directly above difficult kanji characters as a pronunciation aid for children and foreigners, a system known as furigana.

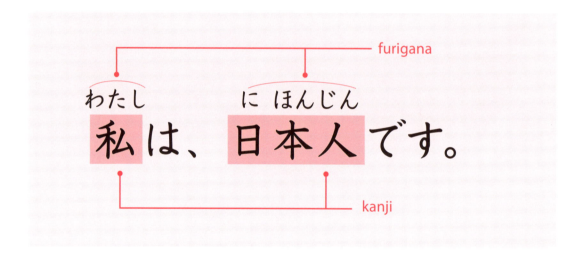

ひらがなの使われ方

　日本語にはひらがな、かたかな、漢字と3つの文字があります。
　「かたかな」は主に外来語につかわれ、漢字は名前や動詞、形容詞の一部として使われます。実は、ひらがなは助詞や動詞、形容詞の一部としてしか使われません。しかし、まだ難しい漢字が分からない子供や外国の方のために、漢字のうえにふりがなとよばれるひらがなを書きます。

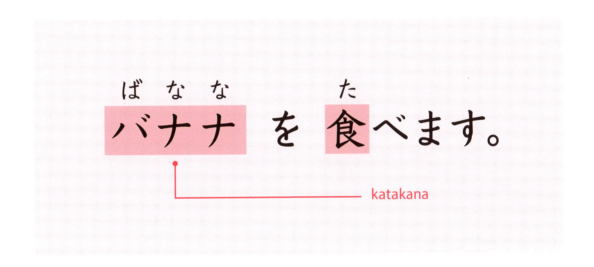

The History of Hiragana

The hiragana script evolved from Chinese characters transmitted to Japan long ago. Although those characters were originally assigned to the different sounds of the Japanese language, around AD 800 they were simplified into hiragana characters which were used mostly by women.

Sometime later, the Iroha was invented to help people remember hiragana, similar to the function of the ABC song in English. The poem was used for many centuries, but around the turn of the twentieth century the 48 hiragana characters learned by elementary school students were standardized and an ordering system which began with あいうえお gained in popularity.

Iroha

> Iro ha nihoheto
> Chirinuru wo
> Wa ka yo tare so
> Tsune naramu
> Uwi no okuyama
> Kefu koete
> Asaki yume mishi
> Wehi mo sesu

(modern translation)
Even the flowers and their brilliant colors
will one day fade away
And even we who inhabit this world
cannot stay the same forever.
Cryptic mountain roads hiding unseen dangers
we traverse them today
But that we can shield our minds from foolish dreams
and our bodies from intoxicating aspirations.

As you can see, the poem has quite a profound meaning.

Though there is no poem to go along with the modern ordering of あいうえお (also known as *gojūon*), I think that the newer system is easier for foreigners studying Japanese to remember since it starts with the vowel sounds. Let's have a look at the hiragana chart on the next page.

ひらがなの歴史

　ひらがなは、漢字からつくられました。
　日本には、中国から伝わってきた漢字があったので、それを日本語の音にあてていましたが、800年頃から漢字を簡素化したひらがなが作られて、主に女性が使いました。
　その後、仮名を覚えるための「いろは歌」がつくられました。英語のABC songのようなもので、長い間使われていましたが、1900年に、小学校で使うひらがな48字が決められて、「あいうえお」からはじまる順が一般に普及しました。

いろは歌

いろはにほへと　ちりぬるを

わかよたれそ　つねならむ

うゐのおくやま　けふこえて

あさきゆめみし　ゑひもせす

（現代語訳）
きれいな色の花もいつか散ってしまう
世を生きる私達も同じ
奥深い山のような世の中を今日もこえて
あさはかな夢など見ないで、
日々を受け入れて行こう

　このように、深い意味があるのです。

　現代の「あいうえお順」（五十音ともいう）は歌ではありませんが、母音のaiueoからはじまっているので、外国人学習者には覚えやすいとおもいます。次のページでひらがな表をみてみましょう。

Japanese Writing and Pronunciation

The hiragana syllabary contains 46 basic characters. Five of these represent vowels (あ, い, う, え, お) which are phonetically combined with consonants to form the remaining characters. In addition, many characters can be modified using the accent marks 「゛」 or 「゜」 to form slightly different sounds. Variants created by appending a small や, ゆ, or よ also exist.

Hiragana

Basic syllables

	a		i		u		e		o	
		あ		い		う		え		お
ka	か	ki	き	ku	く	ke	け	ko	こ
sa	さ	shi	し	su	す	se	せ	so	そ
ta	た	chi	ち	tsu	つ	te	て	to	と
na	な	ni	に	nu	ぬ	ne	ね	no	の
ha/wa	は	hi	ひ	fu	ふ	he/e	へ	ho	ほ
ma	ま	mi	み	mu	む	me	め	mo	も
ya	や			yu	ゆ			yo	よ
ra	ら	ri	り	ru	る	re	れ	ro	ろ
wa	わ							wo/o	を
n	ん								

kya	きゃ	kyu	きゅ	kyo	きょ
sha	しゃ	shu	しゅ	sho	しょ
cha	ちゃ	chu	ちゅ	cho	ちょ
nya	にゃ	nyu	にゅ	nyo	にょ
hya	ひゃ	hyu	ひゅ	hyo	ひょ
mya	みゃ	myu	みゅ	myo	みょ

rya	りゃ	ryu	りゅ	ryo	りょ

Modified syllables

ga	が	gi	ぎ	gu	ぐ	ge	げ	go	ご
za	ざ	ji	じ	zu	ず	ze	ぜ	zo	ぞ
da	だ	ji	ぢ	zu	づ	de	で	do	ど
ba	ば	bi	び	bu	ぶ	be	べ	bo	ぼ
pa	ぱ	pi	ぴ	pu	ぷ	pe	ぺ	po	ぽ

gya	ぎゃ	gyu	ぎゅ	gyo	ぎょ
ja	じゃ	ju	じゅ	jo	じょ

bya	びゃ	byu	びゅ	byo	びょ
pya	ぴゃ	pyu	ぴゅ	pyo	ぴょ

This syllable set is primarily used for words borrowed from other languages, but they are also widely adopted into logos, slang speech, and other formats.

1

Katakana

Basic syllables

a	ア	i	イ	u	ウ	e	エ	o	オ
ka	カ	ki	キ	ku	ク	ke	ケ	ko	コ
sa	サ	shi	シ	su	ス	se	セ	so	ソ
ta	タ	chi	チ	tsu	ツ	te	テ	to	ト
na	ナ	ni	ニ	nu	ヌ	ne	ネ	no	ノ
ha/wa	ハ	hi	ヒ	fu	フ	he/e	ヘ	ho	ホ
ma	マ	mi	ミ	mu	ム	me	メ	mo	モ
ya	ヤ			yu	ユ			yo	ヨ
ra	ラ	ri	リ	ru	ル	re	レ	ro	ロ
wa	ワ							wo/o	ヲ
n	ン								

kya	キャ	kyu	キュ	kyo	キョ
sha	シャ	shu	シュ	sho	ショ
cha	チャ	chu	チュ	cho	チョ
nya	ニャ	nyu	ニュ	nyo	ニョ
hya	ヒャ	hyu	ヒュ	hyo	ヒョ
mya	ミャ	myu	ミュ	myo	ミョ

rya	リャ	ryu	リュ	ryo	リョ

Modified syllables

ga	ガ	gi	ギ	gu	グ	ge	ゲ	go	ゴ
za	ザ	ji	ジ	zu	ズ	ze	ゼ	zo	ゾ
da	ダ	ji	ヂ	zu	ヅ	de	デ	do	ド
ba	バ	bi	ビ	bu	ブ	be	ベ	bo	ボ
pa	パ	pi	ピ	pu	プ	pe	ペ	po	ポ

gya	ギャ	gyu	ギュ	gyo	ギョ
ja	ジャ	ju	ジュ	jo	ジョ

bya	ビャ	byu	ビュ	byo	ビョ
pya	ピャ	pyu	ピュ	pyo	ピョ

Chapter 2

Examples and Practice
Single Characters

第 2 章　ひらがなの書き方
<small>だい に しょう　　　　　　か かた</small>

Lesson 1

Trace over the outlines in the middle row first, then try writing those same characters in the blank boxes below. Refer to the numbers and arrows for guidance on stroke order and direction.

あいうえお　かきくけこ

Lesson 2

Trace over the outlines in the middle row first, then try writing those same characters in the blank boxes below. Refer to the numbers and arrows for guidance on stroke order and direction.

さ行 さ row

た行 た row

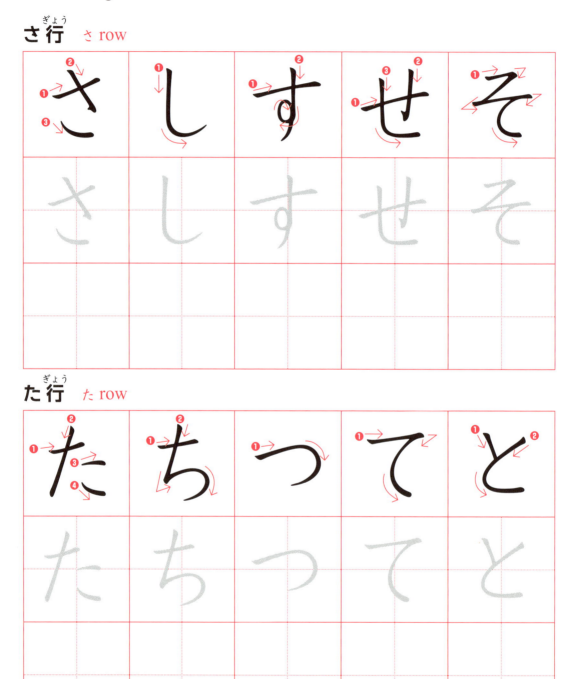

20

Lesson 3

Trace over the outlines in the middle row first, then try writing those same characters in the blank boxes below. Refer to the numbers and arrows for guidance on stroke order and direction.

な row

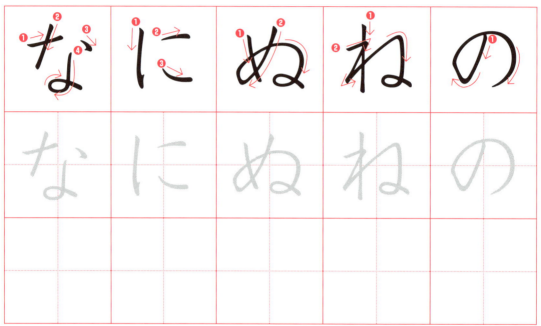

は行 は row

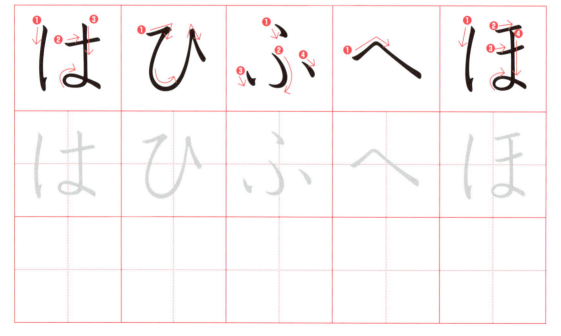

Lesson 4

Trace over the outlines in the middle row first, then try writing those same characters in the blank boxes below. Refer to the numbers and arrows for guidance on stroke order and direction.

 ま row

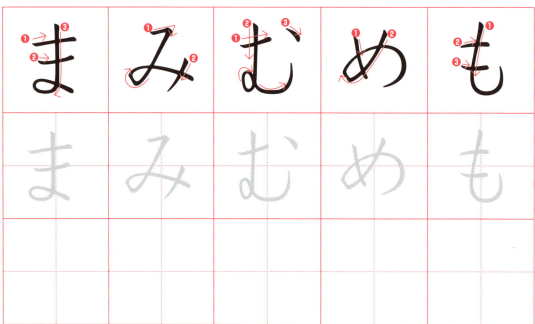

 や row

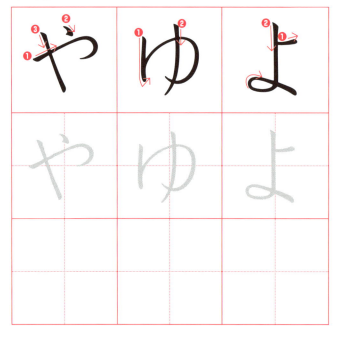

まみむめも　やゆよ

2

Lesson 5

Trace over the outlines in the middle row first, then try writing those same characters in the blank boxes below. Refer to the numbers and arrows for guidance on stroke order and direction.

ら行 ら row

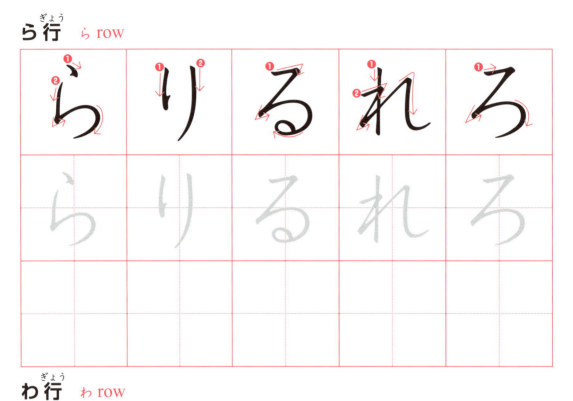

わ行 わ row

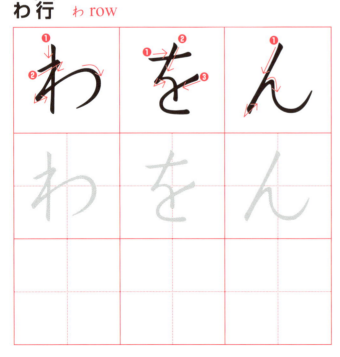

らりるれろ　わをん

wa	ra	u
わ	ら	う

to laugh

wa	su	re	ru
わ	す	れ	る

to forget

ri	su
り	す

squirrel

o
を

object を Verb

object marker

o	ri	ru
お	り	る

get off

ho	n
ほ	ん

book

wa	re	ru
わ	れ	る

to break

hi	ro	i
ひ	ろ	い

spacious

27

Lesson 6

Trace over the outlines in the middle row first, then try writing those same characters in the blank boxes below. Refer to the numbers and arrows for guidance on stroke order and direction.

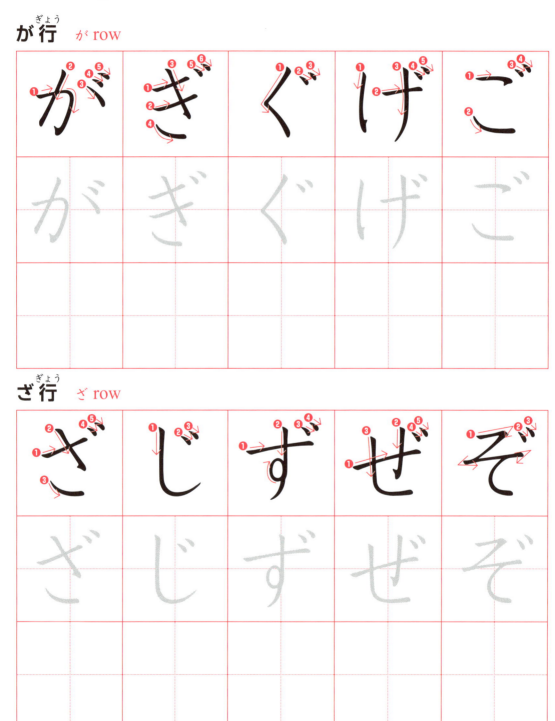

がぎぐげご　ざじずぜぞ

hi ra ga na ひらがな — hiragana

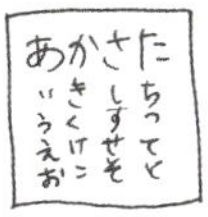

za n ne n ざんねん — unfortunate / shame

gi n ko u ぎんこう — bank

ji ka n じかん — time

mo u su gu もうすぐ — soon

ne zu mi ねずみ — mouse

ge n i n げんいん — cause

ze hi ぜひ — I would love to / by all means

go go ごご — afternoon

zo u ぞう — elephant

Lesson 7

Trace over the outlines in the middle row first, then try writing those same characters in the blank boxes below. Refer to the numbers and arrows for guidance on stroke order and direction.

だ row

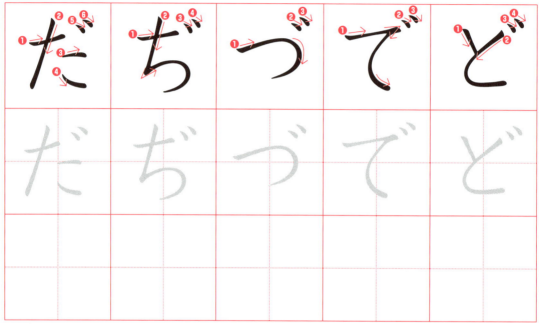

ば行 ば row

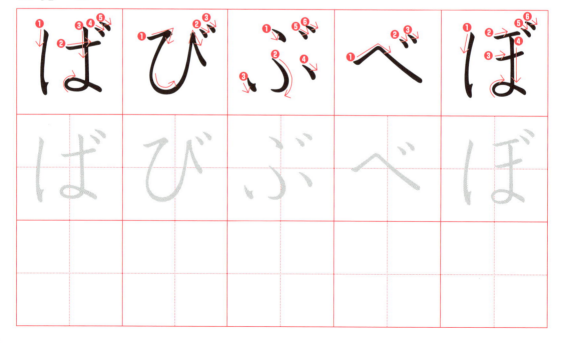

Lesson 8

Trace over the outlines in the middle row first, then try writing those same characters in the blank boxes below. Refer to the numbers and arrows for guidance on stroke order and direction.

ぱ行　ぱ row

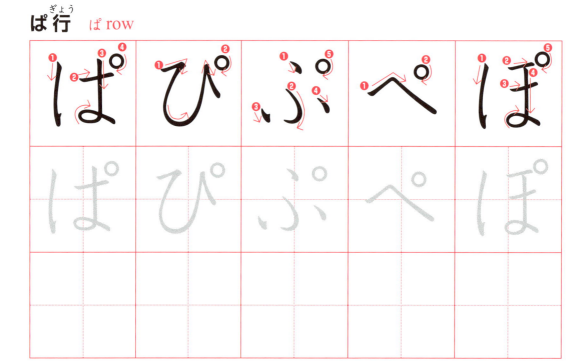

ぱぴぷぺぽ

ka	n	pa	i
か	ん	ぱ	い

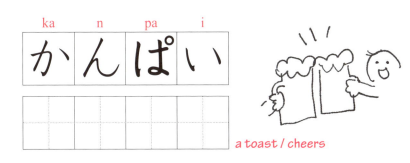
a toast / cheers

shi	n	pi	n
し	ん	ぴ	ん

brand-new

te	n	pu	ra
て	ん	ぷ	ら

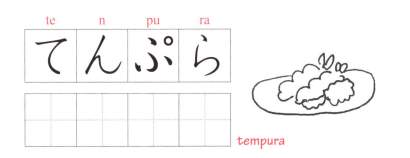
tempura

ka	n	pe	ki
か	ん	ぺ	き

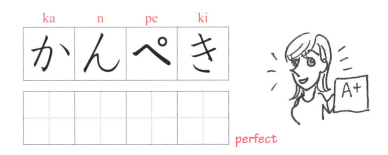
perfect

po	n	ka	n
ぽ	ん	か	ん

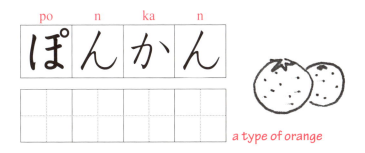
a type of orange

Tricky Characters

These characters have similar shapes, so take extra care when using them.

にている文字

Draw a line between each hiragana character and its romaji equivalent.

I

ち	•	•	mo
い	•	•	a
め	•	•	chi
ら	•	•	shi
あ	•	•	o
し	•	•	nu
お	•	•	i
り	•	•	me
ぬ	•	•	ri
も	•	•	ra

II

ほ	•	•	ki
れ	•	•	sa
す	•	•	nu
き	•	•	ru
る	•	•	mu
は	•	•	ha
さ	•	•	su
ぬ	•	•	re
ろ	•	•	ho
む	•	•	ro

ねこ？
れこ？

Answers can be found on the next page.

Answers

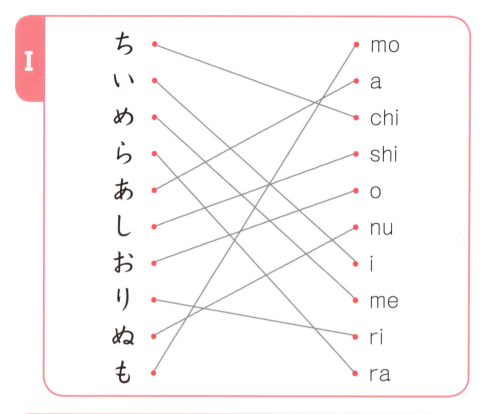

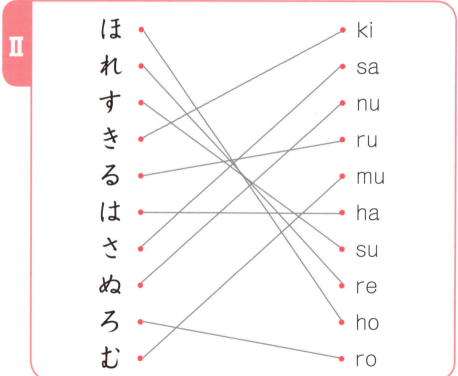

Chapter 3

Examples and Practice

Combinations and Symbols

第 3 章　組み合わせた文字・記号

Lesson 9

When つ is smaller than the characters next to it, it is silent (don't pronounce it). Instead, add a slight pause before saying the next character.

き ki　つ tsu　て te　→　きって ki × tte

In romaji, the presence of a small つ is indicated by a double consonant.

ki	ppu
き	っぷ

train ticket

ki	tto
き	っと

surely / certainly

sa	kki
さ	っき

just now / a while ago

yo	ppa	ra	i
よ	っぱ	ら	い

intoxicated

su	kka	ri
す	っか	り

completely

za	sshi
ざ	っし

magazine

Small っ

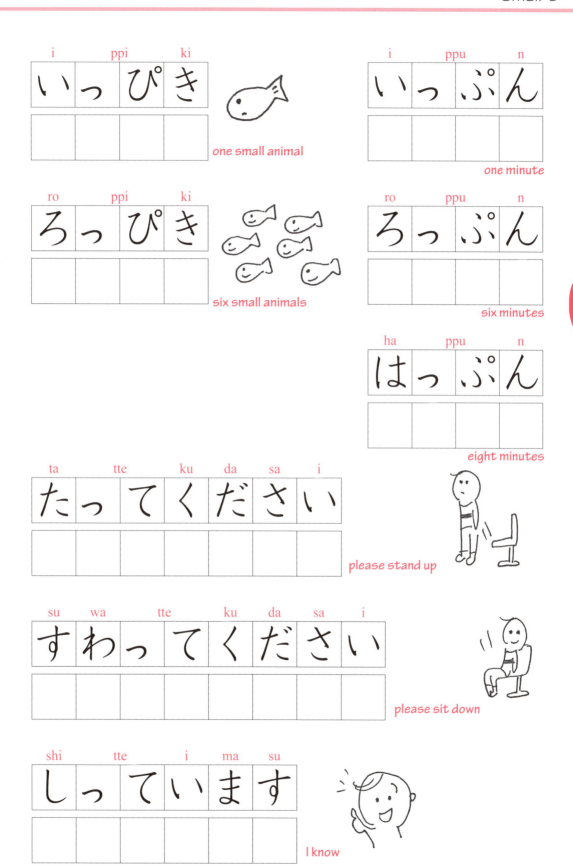

Lesson 10

Unlike the small つ, when a small や, ゆ, or よ follows a character it changes the sound.

き ki や ya → きゃ kya

き ki ゆ yu → きゅ kyu

き ki よ yo → きょ kyo

o	kya	ku	sa	ma
お	きゃ	く	さ	ま

customer / guest

kyu	u	ri
きゅ	う	り

cucumber

kyu	u	ko	u
きゅ	う	こ	う

express train

kyo	u
きょ	う

today

kyo	u	ka	i
きょ	う	か	い

church

きゃきゅきょ　ぎゃぎゅぎょ

ぎ gi や ya → ぎゃ gya

ぎ gi ゆ yu → ぎゅ gyu

ぎ gi よ yo → ぎょ gyo

3

gya ku
ぎゃく

opposite

gyu u ni ku
ぎゅうにく

beef

gyu u gyu u
ぎゅうぎゅう

crammed

ki n gyo
きんぎょ

goldfish

gyo u re tsu
ぎょうれつ

queue / line

41

Lesson 11

As with き and ぎ, a small character from the "Y" row alters the sound of the preceding character.

し shi や ya → しゃ sha

し shi ゆ yu → しゅ shu

し shi よ yo → しょ sho

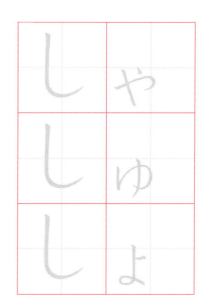

かいしゃいん
ka i sha i n
employee

しゃしん
sha shi n
photograph

しゅじん
shu ji n
husband

しゅうじん
shu u ji n
prisoner

しょうかいする
sho u ka i su ru
to introduce

しょくどう
sho ku do u
cafeteria

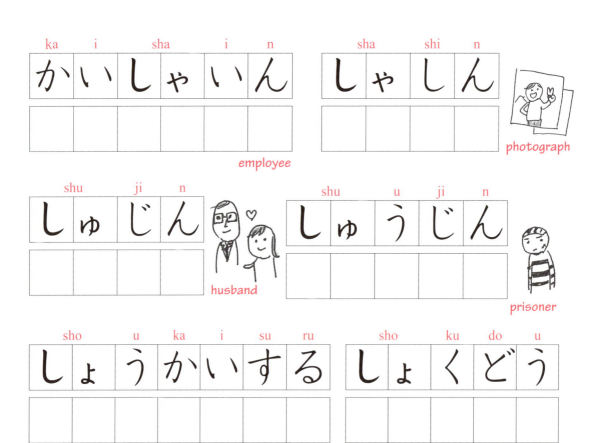

しゃしゅしょ　じゃじゅじょ

じ ji や ya → じゃ ja

じ ji ゆ yu → じゅ ju

じ ji よ yo → じょ jo

3

じゃ ma
じゃま

in the way

ji n ja
じんじゃ

shrine

ju n ba n
じゅんばん

order / sequence

ju gyo u
じゅぎょう

class

jo shi
じょし

girl (mostly used at school)

jo u kyo u
じょうきょう

situation

Lesson 12

ち and に can also be modified by や, ゅ, and ょ.

ち chi や ya → ちゃ cha

ち chi ゅ yu → ちゅ chu

ち chi ょ yo → ちょ cho

o	cha	
お	ちゃ	

Japanese tea

cha	i	ro
ちゃ	い	ろ

brown

chu	u	shi	n
ちゅ	う	し	ん

center

chu	u	go	ku
ちゅ	う	ご	く

China

sha	cho	u
しゃ	ちょ	う

CEO / president

cho	u	shi
ちょ	う	し

condition

ちゃちゅちょ　にゃにゅにょ

に ni　や ya　→　にゃ nya

に ni　ゆ yu　→　にゅ nyu

に ni　よ yo　→　にょ nyo

3

nya	a	nya	a
にゃ	あ	にゃ	あ

sound of cat meowing

gyu	u	nyu	u
ぎゅ	う	にゅ	う

milk

nyu	u	i	n
にゅ	う	い	ん

hospitalization

nyo	u	bo	u
にょ	う	ぼ	う

my wife (originally referred to female servants in the Heian period)

Lesson 13

Other characters which can be modified by the "Y" row are ひ and び...

ひ hi や ya → ひゃ hya

ひ hi ゆ yu → ひゅ hyu

ひ hi よ yo → ひょ hyo

hya	ku
ひゃ	く

one hundred

ni	hya	ku
に	ひゃ	く

two hundred

hyu	ru	hyu	ru
ひゅ	る	ひゅ	る

used to describe long and wavy shapes

hyo	ro	hyo	ro
ひょ	ろ	ひょ	ろ

used to describe tall and skinny people

ひゃひゅひょ　びゃびゅびょ

び bi や ya → びゃ bya

び bi ゆ yu → びゅ byu

び bi よ yo → びょ byo

3

sa	n	bya	ku
さ	ん	びゃ	く

three hundred

bya	ku	ya
びゃ	く	や

midnight sun

byu	u	byu	u
びゅ	う	びゅ	う

the sound of a hard wind

byo	u	ki
びょ	う	き

illness / sickness

byo	u	i	n
びょ	う	い	ん

hospital

Lesson 14

...as well as ぴ (rarely) and み.

ぴ pi　や ya　→　ぴゃ pya

ぴ pi　ゆ yu　→　ぴゅ pyu

ぴ pi　よ yo　→　ぴょ pyo

ro	っ	ppya	ku
ろ	っ	ぴゃ	く

six hundred

ha	っ	ppya	ku
は	っ	ぴゃ	く

eight hundred

pyu　u　pyu　u
ぴゅ　う　ぴゅ　う

the sound of a whistling wind

ka	n	pyo	u	ma	ki
か	ん	ぴょ	う	ま	き

a type of sushi roll

ぴゃぴゅぴょ　みゃみゅみょ

み mi　や ya　→　みゃ mya

み mi　ゆ yu　→　みゅ myu

み mi　よ yo　→　みょ myo

mya	ku
みゃ	く

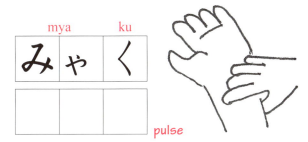

pulse

kya	rī	pa	myu	pa	myu
きゃ	りー	ぱ	みゅ	ぱ	みゅ

name of a Japanese pop star

ki	myo	u
き	みょ	う

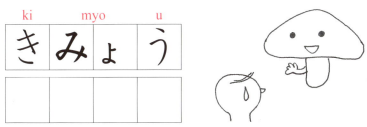

strange / bizarre

Lesson 15

Finally, the sound of り can also be altered by a "Y" character.

り ri や ya → りゃ rya

り ri ゆ yu → りゅ ryu

り ri よ yo → りょ ryo

rya	ku
りゃ	く

 Mac / Misdo

abbreviation

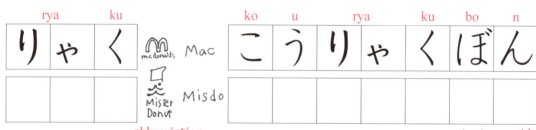

strategy guide

exchange/international student

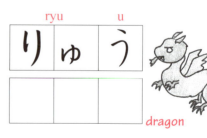

dragon

cuisine

trip

In addition, や/ゆ/よ can be combined with っ, and the result is as you would expect: the normal "Y-modified" sound followed by a slight pause. The best way to practice this combination is by saying each sound slowly and carefully to avoid smearing the sounds together. And when writing any of these small characters by hand, make sure that they are small enough to be distinguishable from their larger versions—otherwise the result can be difficult to decipher.

ち ch + や (ya) + つ (tsu) た ta
→ ちゃった cha × tta

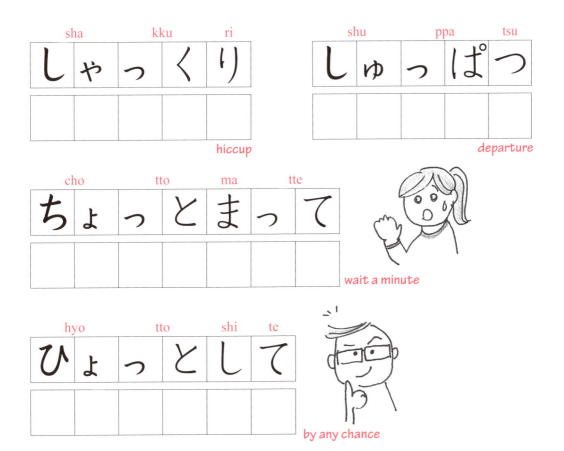

しゃっくり — sha kku ri — hiccup

しゅっぱつ — shu ppa tsu — departure

ちょっとまって — cho tto ma tte — wait a minute

ひょっとして — hyo tto shi te — by any chance

Lesson 16

When う follows another character, it extends that character's vowel sound—simply hold it for a slightly longer duration. In romaji, this is typically denoted with a horizontal line over the vowel.

ふ fu + う u → ふう fū

ū

fū fu
ふ う ふ
married couple

sū ji
す う じ
numbers

fū se n
ふ う せ ん
balloon

kyū ka
き ゅ う か
vacation

gyū nyū
ぎ ゅ う に ゅ う
milk

Extended Vowels

father

why

park

hat / cap

cooking / cuisine

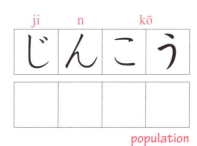
population

cleaning

parent

salary

Lesson 17

かっこ
Quotation marks

He said "wait."

一　長音符
　ちょうおんぷ

This horizonal line is not traditionally used in hiragana, but in recent times it has become popular in informal writing. It signifies an extended vowel sound.

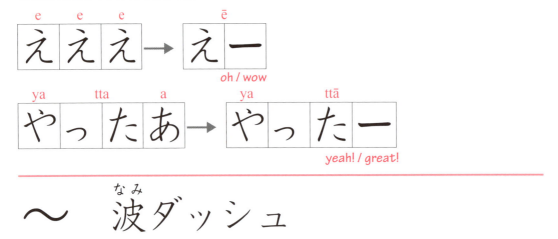

〜　波ダッシュ
　　なみ

Often used to indicate a range (such as times or dates). This wavy line can also extend the vowel sound that precedes it, but it does so less forcefully than the straight horizontal line.

from Tokyo to Osaka

can serve as a placeholder (similar to a blank line in English)

____ please.

Lesson 18

Punctuation 、 。

In Japanese, *ten* is sometimes placed after the particle that immediately follows the subject. In general, its role is the same as the English comma: to indicate a slight pause. *Maru* marks the end of a sentence.

ten 、 comma

maru 。 period

Today is sunny.

Ten also comes after conjunctions.

It's sunny, but cold.

56

Chapter 4

Main Types of Hiragana Words

第 4 章　主にひらがなが使われる言葉

Lesson 19

Greetings and other common set phrases are written in hiragana. Note that the は found at the end of greeting phrases is pronounced "wa" and not "ha."

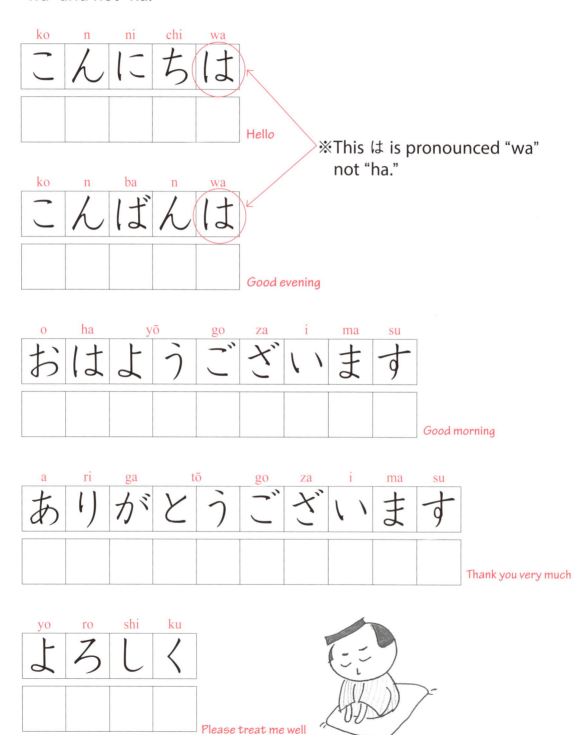

Greetings and Set Phrases

i	ta	da	ki	ma	su
い	た	だ	き	ま	す

(said before eating)

go	chi	sō	sa	ma	de	shi	ta
ご	ち	そ	う	さ	ま	で	し	た

(said after eating)

4

su	mi	ma	se	n
す	み	ま	せ	ん

I'm sorry (formal)

go	me	n	na	sa	i
ご	め	ん	な	さ	い

I'm sorry (casual)

ma	ta
ま	た

see you later

sa	yō	na	ra
さ	よ	う	な	ら

goodbye

Lesson 20

[Particles 1]   は, が, を, へ

1

As a particle, は is pronounced "wa," not "ha." This は marks the topic* of the sentence.

2

This particle is a subject* marker. It is used when the subject of the sentence needs to be explicitly specified from among a number of possibilities.

Particles 1: は, が, を, へ

3

本 を 読みます。
Hon o yomi masu. *(I) read books.*

を is pronounced the same as お but is only used as a particle to mark the object of the sentence. ます is a verb suffix and always appears in hiragana. (Subjects are often omitted when they are mutually understood from the context.)

4

学校 へ 行きます。
Gakkō e iki masu. *(I'll) head toward the school.*

As a particle, へ is pronounced "eh." This へ is roughly equivalent to the English *toward* or *to*.

*While an in-depth discussion of the differences between は and が is beyond the scope of the book, don't get discouraged if you struggle with using them correctly. Mastering their usage requires a lot of exposure and practice.

Lesson 21

[Particles 2]　で, に, と, から, まで

1

This particle has several uses. It marks the place where an action occurs, similar to "at" or "in" in English. で can also be used to mark the thing that is used to perform an action or task, a usage which corresponds closely to with or by.

2

When used between a person and a noun, の indicates possession.

3

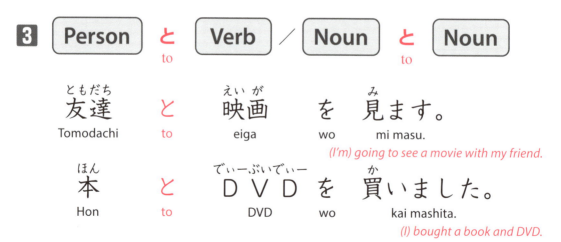

When と connects a person and an action verb, it indicates the action is done together with that person. But when と comes between two nouns, it just means and.

Particles 2: で, に, と, から, まで

4 Time/Date に / Place に Verb
　　　　　　　　ni　　　　　　　ni

１月 に
ichigatsu ni — *in January*

２時 に
niji ni — *at 2 o'clock*

学校 に 行きました。
Gakkō ni iki mashita. — *(He) went to school.*

に can connect a place with a verb to indicate a destination. It is also used after dates and times.

5 Date/Time/Place/Person から
　　　　　　　　　　　　　　kara

中国 から 来ました。
Chūgoku kara ki mashita. — *(I) come from China.*

火曜日 から
kayōbi kara — *from Tuesday*

から is equivalent to the English "from" and is used in a wide variety of situations.

6 Place/Date/Time まで
　　　　　　　　　　　made

駅 まで お願いします。
Eki made onegai shimasu. — *To the station, please.*

大阪 から 東京 まで
Ōsaka kara Tōkyō made — *from Osaka to Tokyo*

まで means until or to and is often used in combination with から to express a range of time or distance.

Lesson 22

Most question words are written in hiragana, but 何 (なに) generally appears as kanji. だれ can also be written in kanji (誰), although hiragana is usually used for advertisements and other applications that require a softer and more casual appearance.

1 どこ／どちら *where / which*
（do ko / do chi ra）

駅（えき）はどこですか。
Eki wa do ko de su ka? *Where is the station?*

どちらからですか。
Do chi ra ka ra de su ka? *Which (place) are you from?*

※ Japanese doesn't technically have a question mark, but recently its use has become common in casual writing.

2 いつ *when*
（i tsu）

いつですか。
I tsu de su ka. *When is it?*

いつでもいいです。
I tsu de mo i i de su. *Anytime is fine.*

Question Words

3 なんで／どうして *why (casual) / why (formal)*
na n de / do u shi te

なんで勉強してるの？
Na n de ben kyō shi te ru no? *Why are you study?*

どうして勉強してるの？
Do u shi te ben kyō shi te ru no? *Why are you study?*

4 どうやって *how*
do u ya tte

どうやって使いますか。
Do u ya tte tsuka i ma su ka? *How do you use (it)?*

5 どのくらい *how long*
do no ku ra i

どのくらいかかりますか。
Do no ku ra i ka ka ri ma su ka? *How long will it take?*

6 だれ／どなた *who / who (formal)*
da re / do na ta

だれが来る？
Da re ga ku ru? *Who is coming?*

どなたですか。
Do na ta de su ka? *Who is it?*

Lesson 23

For the most part, connecting words in Japanese are used just as they are in English. They are always written in hiragana.

1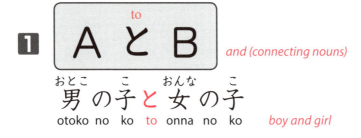

and (connecting nouns)

男の子と女の子
otoko no ko to onna no ko   boy and girl

2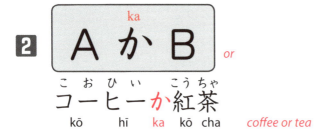

or

コーヒーか紅茶
kō hī ka kō cha   coffee or tea

3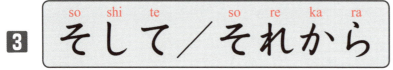

and (connecting sentences) / next; and then

砂糖をいれます。そして[それから]醤油もいれます。
Sa tō o i re ma su.   So shi te / So re ka ra   shō yu mo i re ma su.

Add the sugar then the soy sauce also.

4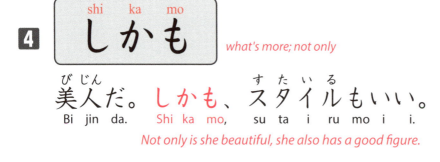

what's more; not only

美人だ。しかも、スタイルもいい。
Bi jin da.   Shi ka mo, su ta i ru mo i i.

Not only is she beautiful, she also has a good figure.

5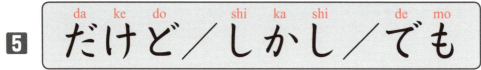

although; but (casual) / but (formal) / but (casual)

Connecting Words

あの人変だけど、好き。
A no hito hen da ke do, su ki. *That guy is weird, but I like him.*

一生懸命がんばった。しかし[でも]、負けてしまった。
Isshō ken mei ga n ba tta. Shi ka shi / De mo, ma ke te shi ma tta.
I tried my best, but I failed.

6 だから／なので
da ka ra / na no de

because; so (casual) / because; so (formal)

雨だから、行かない。
Ame da ka ra, i ka na i. *It's raining so I won't go.*

病気なので、行けません。
Byō ki na no de, i ke ma se n. *I can't go because I'm sick.*

6 ところで／そういえば
to ko ro de / so u i e ba

by the way / speaking of

ところで、この話を知ってますか？
To ko ro de, ko no hanashi o shi tte ma su ka?
By the way, do you know this story?

A: 田中さんに会いたいね。
Ta naka sa n ni a i ta i ne. *I want to meet Tanaka.*

B: そういえば、あの人結婚したそうですよ。
So u i e ba, a no hito kekkon shi ta sō de su yo.
Speaking of him, I heard he got married.

7 それにしても
in any case; even so

それにしても、大変だ。
So re ni shi te mo, tai hen da. *In any case, it will be very difficult.*

Lesson 24

Adverbs are another category of words that is always written in hiragana. And just as in English, they are used to modify verbs, adjectives, and other adverbs.

1  very (formal) / very (casual)

とてもきれいです。
To te mo ki re i de su.   (It) is very beautiful.

すごくおいしい。
Su go ku o i shi i.   (It) is very delicious.

2  often, well / not really, not so much

よくできました！
Yo ku de ki ma shi ta!   Well done!

あまりすきじゃないです。
A ma ri su ki ja na i de su.   I don't like (that) so much.

Adverbs

3 たまに／いつも （ta ma ni／i tsu mo） *rarely / always*

たまに美術館に行く。
Ta ma ni bi jutsu kan ni i ku.   *I rarely go to art museums.*

いつもひまです。
I tsu mo hi ma de su.   *I'm always free.*

4 ゆっくり／のんびり （yu kku ri／no n bi ri） *slowly / leisurely*

彼女はゆっくり話す。
Kano jo wa yu kku ri hana su.   *She speaks slowly.*

のんびり仕事してる。
No n bi ri shi goto shi te ru.   *I'm working leisurely.*

69

Lesson 25

Ideophones modify verbs and adverbs, providing vivid descriptions related to color, texture, and many other attributes. The most well-known of these are onomatopoeia words, which represent sounds. While the English language also contains some ideophones (a dog says woof-woof, for example), they pale in comparison to the many thousands that exist in Japanese.
These words are nearly written in kana (either hiragana or katakana, depending on the stylistic goal of text).

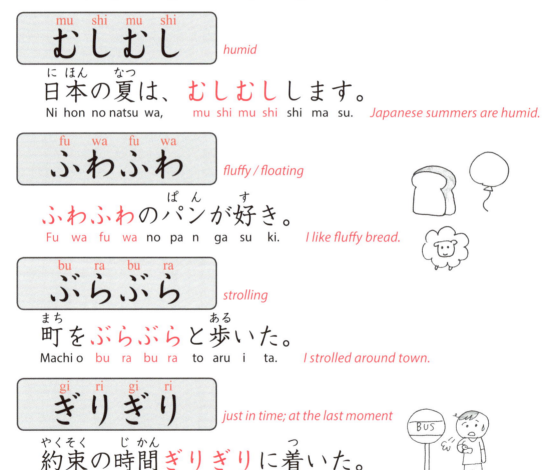

むしむし (mu shi mu shi) — *humid*

日本の夏は、むしむしします。
Ni hon no natsu wa, mu shi mu shi shi ma su. — *Japanese summers are humid.*

ふわふわ (fu wa fu wa) — *fluffy / floating*

ふわふわのパンが好き。
Fu wa fu wa no pa n ga su ki. — *I like fluffy bread.*

ぶらぶら (bu ra bu ra) — *strolling*

町をぶらぶらと歩いた。
Machi o bu ra bu ra to aru i ta. — *I strolled around town.*

ぎりぎり (gi ri gi ri) — *just in time; at the last moment*

約束の時間ぎりぎりに着いた。
Yaku soku no ji kan gi ri gi ri ni tsu i ta. — *I arrived just in time for my appointment.*

ばくばく (ba ku ba ku) — *eating sound*

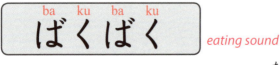

おいしくて、ばくばく食べちゃう！
O i shi ku te, ba ku ba ku ta be cha u! — *It is so good, I'm gobbling it right up!*

Ideophones

ごくごく (go ku go ku) — *drinking sound*

赤(あか)ちゃんがミルク(みるく)をごくごく飲(の)んでる。
Aka chan ga miruku o goku goku nonderu.
The baby is gulping down his milk.

きょろきょろ (kyo ro kyo ro) — *look around*

きょろきょろして、どうしたの？
Kyoro kyoro shite, dou shita no?
Why are you looking around?

どたばた (do ta ba ta) — *noisily; make noise*

どたばたしないで！
Dotabata shinai de!
Don't stomp around.

そろそろ (so ro so ro) — *steadily approaching (in terms of time)*

そろそろ失礼(しつれい)します。
Soro soro shitsurei shimasu.
It's about time to leave.

ぺらぺら (pe ra pe ra) — *speak fluently*

日本語(にほんご)がぺらぺらですね！
Nihongo ga pera pera desu ne!
Your Japanese is very fluent!

のろのろ (no ro no ro) — *slowly; sluggishly*

亀(かめ)がのろのろ歩(ある)いている。
Kame ga noro noro aruite iru.
The turtle is walking slowly.

ぺちゃくちゃ (pe cha ku cha) — *to chit-chat, especially in an animated manner*

おばさんたちがぺちゃくちゃ話(はな)してる。
Obasan tachi ga pecha kucha hanashiteru.
Those ladies are chatting excitedly.

Chapter 5

Reading Exercises and the Vertical Style

第 5 章　読む練習・縦書きの練習

Reading Exercise

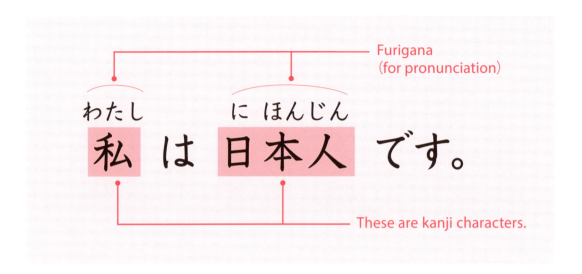

Read the following sentences.

1 <ruby>明日<rt>あした</rt></ruby>は<ruby>雨<rt>あめ</rt></ruby>です。

2 <ruby>昨日<rt>きのう</rt></ruby>は<ruby>晴<rt>は</rt></ruby>れでした。

3 <ruby>私<rt>わたし</rt></ruby>は<ruby>元気<rt>げんき</rt></ruby>です。

Romaji / *English translation*

1 Ashita wa ame desu. / *It will rain tomorrow.*

2 Kinō wa hare deshita. / *Yesterday was sunny.*

3 Watashi wa genki desu. / *I'm feeling fine.*

Adding Kanji

4 <ruby>桜<rt>さくら</rt></ruby>はきれいですね。

5 <ruby>富士山<rt>ふじさん</rt></ruby>は<ruby>高<rt>たか</rt></ruby>いですか。

6 <ruby>僕<rt>ぼく</rt></ruby>は<ruby>大学生<rt>だいがくせい</rt></ruby>です。

7 <ruby>彼女<rt>かのじょ</rt></ruby>はかわいいけど、こわいです。

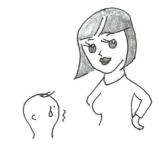

8 <ruby>納豆<rt>なっとう</rt></ruby>はねばねばだから、<ruby>好<rt>す</rt></ruby>きじゃないです。

---

4 Sakura wa kirei desu ne. / *Cherry blossoms are beautiful.*
5 Fujisan wa takai desu ka? / *Is Mt. Fuji tall?*
6 Boku wa daigakusei desu. / *I'm a college student.*
7 Kanojo wa kawaii kedo, kowai desu. / *My girlfriend is cute but scary.*
8 Nattō wa nebaneba dakara, suki janai desu / *I don't like natto because it's gooey.*

Reading Exercise

Read the following sentences.

1 焼(や)き肉(にく)を食べました。

2 牛乳(ぎゅうにゅう)を飲(の)みました。

3 本(ほん)を読(よ)みますか。

4 映画(えいが)を見(み)るつもりです。

5 日曜日(にちようび)の朝(あさ)、海(うみ)へ行(い)きました。

Romaji / *English translation*

1 Yakiniku o tabe mashita. / *I ate some yakiniku. (Japanese B.B.Q)*
2 Gyūnyū o nomimashita. / *I drank some milk.*
3 Hon o yomi masu ka? / *Do you read books?*
4 Eiga o miru tsumori desu. / *I'm going to see a movie.*
5 Nichiyōbi no asa, umi e iki mashita. / *Sunday morning, I went to the sea.*

Adding Kanji

6 部屋へ入ってください。
　　へや　　はい

7 私は東京に住んでいます。
　　わたし　とうきょう　す

8 姉は京都で働いています。
　　あね　きょうと　はたら

9 かわいい女の子を見た。
　　　　　おんな　こ　み

10 一緒に音楽を聞こう。
　　いっしょ　おんがく　き

11 学校で日本語を勉強しています。
　　がっこう　にほんご　べんきょう

5

6　Heya e haitte kudasai. / *Please come in my room.*
7　Watashi wa Tōkyō ni sunde imasu. / *I live in Tokyo.*
8　Ane wa Kyōto de hataraite imasu. / *My elder sister works in Kyoto.*
9　Kawaii onnanoko o mita. / *I saw a cute girl.*
10　Issho ni ongaku o kikou. / *Let's listen to music together.*
11　Gakkō de nihongo o benkyō shite imasu. / *I'm studying Japanese at school.*

Reading Exercise

Katakana is used for Western words and so it often uses the horizontal line. This line denotes an extended vowel sound. (See p. 54)

す　　う　　ぱ　　あ
ス　ー　パ　ー
sū　　　　pā
　　　　　　　super

Read the following sentences.

1 タクシーに乗った。
　　た く し い　　の

2 ケーキとコーヒーはいかがですか。
　　け え き　　こ お ひ い

Romaji / *English translation*
1 Takushī ni notta. / *I took a taxi.*
2 Kēki to kōhī wa ikaga desu ka? / *Would you like some cake and coffee?*

Adding Katakana

3 <ruby>スプーン<rt>すぷうん</rt></ruby>と<ruby>フォーク<rt>ふぉおく</rt></ruby>をください。

4 <ruby>ハンバーガー<rt>はんばあがあ</rt></ruby>が<ruby>食<rt>た</rt></ruby>べたい。

5 お<ruby>父<rt>とう</rt></ruby>さんと<ruby>キャッチボール<rt>きゃっちぼおる</rt></ruby>をした。

いくぞっ
(Here goes!)

6 <ruby>インド<rt>いんど</rt></ruby>に<ruby>行<rt>い</rt></ruby>って、<ruby>ゾウ<rt>ぞう</rt></ruby>にのった。

----

3 Spūn to fōku o kudasai. / A spoon and fork, please.
4 Hanbāgā ga tabetai. / I want to eat a hamburger.
5 Otōsan to kyatchi bōru o shita. / I played catch with my dad.
6 Indo ni itte, zō ni notta. / I went to India and rode an elephant.

Reading Exercise

Read the following sentences.

A 今日は金よう日。仕事の後、彼とおしゃれなバーに行く予定。楽しみ〜。わくわく。残業がないといいな。

B やっと仕事が休み！今日はどこにも行かないで家で一日中ゲームをしよう。

Romaji / English translation

A Kyō wa kinyōbi. Shigoto no ato, kare to oshare na bā ni iku yotei. Tanoshimī. Waku waku. Zangyō ga nai to ii na.

Today is Friday. I'm going to a fancy bar with my boyfriend after work. Exciting! I hope I won't have to work overtime.

B Yatto shigoto ga yasumi! Kyō wa doko ni mo ikanaide uchi de ichinichijū gēmu o shiyō.

Finally I got a day off. I'll stay home and play video games all day!

Longer Passages

C 毎朝6時に起きて、犬の散歩をしている。いつものコースでかわいい女の子に会う。昨日、「おはようございます」と彼女が言った。はじめてだった。どきどきした。

5

c Maiasa rokuji ni okite, inu no sanpo o shiteiru. Itsumo no kōsu de kawaii onnanoko ni au. Kinou, "ohayō gozaimasu" to kanojo ga itta. Hajimete datta. Dokidoki shita.

I wake up at six every morning and walk my dog. On my usual route, I always run into this cute girl. Yesterday she said "Good morning" to me for the first time. I was nervous.

Reading Exercise

Traditional Japanese is written vertically from right to left. This style is almost always used for calligraphy, literature, newspapers, and formal letters (though not business correspondence). Due to their nature, Web sites display Japanese text in the same directions as English.

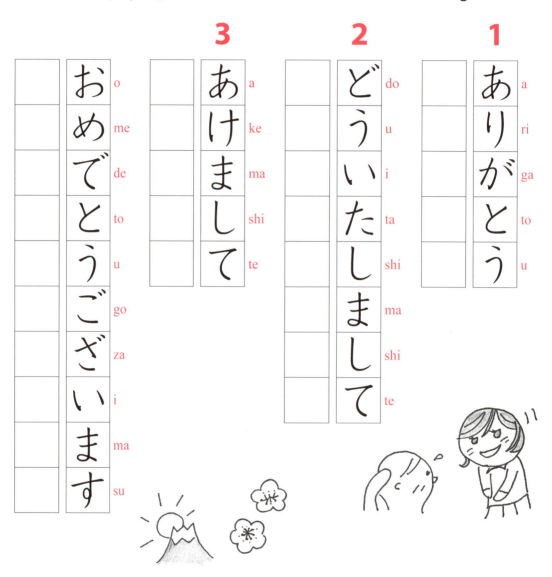

English translation

1 thank you   2 you're welcome   3 Happy New Year

Vertical Writing Style

1. すっぱい (su-ppa-i)
2. びょういん (byo-u-i-n)
3. いらっしゃいませ。 (i-ra-ssha-i-ma-se)
4. ちょっとまってください。 (cho-tto-ma-tte-ku-da-sa-i)
5. しょうゆはしょっぱい。 (sho-u-yu-wa-sho-ppa-i)

1 sour **2** hospital **3** Welcome! **4** Just a moment.
5 Soy sauce is salty.

Reading Exercise

Let's see how well you can read the following excerpt from a fairy tale.

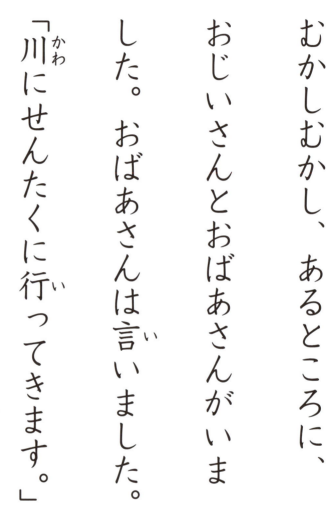

むかしむかし、あるところに、おじいさんとおばあさんがいました。おばあさんは言いました。「川(かわ)にせんたくに行ってきます。」

Romaji / *English translation*

Mukashi mukashi, aru tokoro ni, ojīsan to obāsan ga imashita. Obāsan wa iimashita. "Kawa ni sentaku ni itte kimasu."

Long ago, there lived an old man and woman. One day, the old woman said, "I'm going to the river to do laundry."

Stories and Correspondence

Here is a simple thank-you letter written in polite form.

先日は、お菓子をありがとうございました。家族でおいしくいただきました。またこちらに来たら、ぜひお寄り下さい。

Senjitsu wa, okashi o arigatō gozaimashita. Kazoku de oishiku itadaki mashita. Mata kochira ni kitara, zehi o-yori kudasai.

Thank you for the snacks the other day. The whole family enjoyed eating them very much. Next time you are in the neighborhood, be sure to stop by and see us.

Reading Exercise

See how well you do at reading this famous poem by Miyazawa Kenji and the two haiku that follow it. These haiku in particular are well-known abroad.

宮沢　賢治（みやざわ　けんじ）

雨（あめ）にも負（ま）けず
風（かぜ）にも負（ま）けず
雪（ゆき）にも夏（なつ）の暑（あつ）さにも負（ま）けぬ
じょうぶな体（からだ）をもち
欲（よく）はなく
けっしておこらず
いつもしずかに笑（わら）っている
（中略）
そんな人（ひと）に私（わたし）はなりたい

— Miyazawa Kenji

Unyielding to the rain,
unyielding to the wind
and to the snow and heat of summer.
Maintaining a healthy body
and casting off desire,
avoiding anger always
and forever smiling softly.
(omitted)
I want to be such a person.

Poetry

古池や
蛙飛び込む
水の音

松尾 芭蕉

名月を
とってくれろと
泣く子かな

小林 一茶

old pond
a frog leaps in
splash!

— Matsuo Bashō

harvest moon
"fetch it for me"
cries the child

— Kobayashi Issa

Reading Exercise

Manga is written vertically (although the frames themselves are actually ordered from right to left successively on a given page). Here is a short manga known as a *yon-koma manga* or "four-frame manga."

I am an alien.

huh

Manga

Fish: *Hey frog, let's play!*
Frog: *I don't want to do anything now.*

Fish: *How about drawing?*
Frog: *I really don't want to do anything.*

Fish: *Okay, then, let's play "do nothing."*

glug-glug

EASY AND FUN
HIRAGANA

2017年 4月 5日 第1刷発行
2025年 3月 3日 第4刷発行

著者　小川　清美
発行者　賀川　洋
発行所　IBCパブリッシング株式会社
〒162-0804 東京都新宿区中里町29番3号 菱秀神楽坂ビル
Tel. 03-3513-4511　Fax. 03-3513-4512
www.ibcpub.co.jp

印刷所　中央精版印刷株式会社

© 小川清美2017
Printed in Japan

落丁本・乱丁本は、小社宛にお送りください。送料小社負担にてお取り替えいたします。
本書の無断複写（コピー）は著作権法上での例外を除き禁じられています。

ISBN978-4-7946-0472-9